THE NEWNHAM YEAR

The Inside Perspective

Photography by Alan Davidson

Diary by Dr Catherine Seville

The Newnham Year: The Inside Perspective

© Newnham College, Cambridge and Third Millennium Information Ltd
First published in 2011 by Third Millennium Publishing Limited,
a subsidiary of Third Millennium Information Limited.

2–5 Benjamin Street
London
United Kingdom
ECIM 5QL

www.tmiltd.com

ISBN 978 1 906507 62 6

Photography by Alan Davidson
Designed by Matthew Wilson
Production by Bonnie Murray
Reprographics by Studio Fasoli, Italy
Printed by Printer Trento, Italy

THIRD MILLENNIUM
PUBLISHING. LONDON

Contents

Foreword by Patricia Hodgson   4

MICHAELMAS TERM   6

LENT TERM   72

EASTER TERM   112

Coming up	14
Matriculation	22
College (Newcomers') Feast	30
Settling in	34
Getting down to work	52
Sports	56
Christmas and festivities	62

Literary archive launch	78
Pudding seminars	80
Associates' workshops	81
Visiting speakers	82
Library, archives and special collections	86
Halfway Hall	92
College governance and committees	94
Reaching out to the future	97
Telephone campaign	98
Commemoration	100
Music and drama	106
At work in the gardens	108

Revision and exams	122
Behind the scenes	128
May Week	132
Graduation	134

List of Subscribers	142

Foreword

What do you see in your mind's eye when you think of Newnham? I see strands of autumn mist across the gardens at the start of the Michaelmas term, or the memory of a guest night in the arrangement of chairs and empty glasses in the SCR, or sunshine on the red bricks and windows of Clough Hall at the graduation brunch.

The cycle of the Newnham year has a timeless quality. I was struck, on returning as Principal so many years after I had graduated, by all that had changed and by all that was familiar. Gate hours were only a memory; students gathered in the smart new buttery, not in their separate halls; the 1960s library had been replaced by one that extends and, with modern elegance, pays due homage to the distinguished Yates Thompson core. And that symbolised what was so striking; how well the new builds on the old to bring up to date all that is essentially Newnham. Thus the buildings reflect the character of the community, enriched by each generation that lives and studies here and always true to the original Newnham spirit. Alan Davidson has caught the essence of this special place in the intimate photographs he has taken over the last twelve months. Whilst the faces may not be familiar, the activities and scenes resonate; they bring back sensations and feelings that I am sure we have all experienced at whatever time we were here.

Our Senior Members are the heart of the College community and I am most grateful that our Vice-Principal has opened her diary to allow us an insider's view of many aspects of life at Newnham as a Fellow. Her words provide a glimpse of what it is like for many of our Senior Members as they juggle interviewing, teaching, working on committees to run the College and carrying out research. Whilst Dr Catherine Seville's field is legal, similar stories could be told by many others teaching in a wide range of subjects from Classics to Natural Sciences; from Anglo Saxon Norse and Celtic to Medicine; from Modern and Medieval Languages to History.

Photographs and captions submitted by our alumnae, as well as some of our wonderful archive pictures, add to the contemporary photos to create a collage of faces and reflection of life here over many years.

As we mark the 140th year of the founding of Newnham we can all be proud to have been part of a College that holds a special role in educating generations of young women. The Newnham Network and Community is truly something to be celebrated and I am delighted that so many of our alumnae have participated in this exciting project. The book provides a fascinating insight and I hope you enjoy reading it as much as we have all enjoyed putting it together for you.

Patricia Hodgson DBE
Principal of Newnham College

MICHAELMAS TERM

Dr Catherine Seville (NC 1984) *is the Vice-Principal of Newnham, University Senior Lecturer in Law and Director of Studies. Here she opens her diary to record from her perspective, at the heart of College life, the passage of the Newnham year.*

27th September

Late September, and the excitement and energy are building as the Michaelmas Term approaches. The Long Vacation is never as long or empty as everyone imagines, and there is some regret that research must be restricted for a while. Yet it will be good to see the students, and to begin teaching again. Those returning will be full of plans, and often express pleasure at how at home they now feel in Newnham, whilst recalling the apprehension they felt on arrival. There is so much to be done for the first time, so much local language to learn; and the pace is phenomenal. Like a number of other Directors of Studies I now run a web-based course for the incoming lawyers, in an attempt to make the unfamiliar just a little bit familiar, and to reassure them that they are indeed up to the intellectual pace. This begins as soon as possible after the A-level results are confirmed, and gives a real taste of what to expect. I sense some surprise

from the candidates, who are used to school terms and reading lists which they can always finish, and unused to writing without a pre-defined structure. In spite of my encouragement to express themselves honestly on the course web forum, they write politely there, and (I later learn) share their true feelings only on Facebook!

Miss Clough and the first five students arrived in Cambridge in the autumn of 1871. Women had been able to study for the Cambridge Local Examinations since 1864, but had to take their own lodgings. One of these five, Mary Kennedy, described her earlier installation in a tiny bedroom in a girls' boarding school overlooking Parker's Piece, knowing no one except her brother at Corpus, who was so annoyed at her venture that he would not speak to her. Although she found the lectures 'absorbingly interesting', she found the regime at the boarding-school 'austere and dull'. Henry Sidgwick perceived the need for a proper residential base for women students, and generously rented a house at 74 Regent Street for this purpose, putting Miss Clough in charge. Sharply aware that good reputation was crucial to the venture, Miss Clough was something of a disciplinarian. After Mary Paley and Mary

Kennedy spent a relaxed day in Ely, even climbing the cathedral tower 'in the company of a young man', a rule requiring the Principal's permission for 'excursions' was instituted. Although students today are bound by different social conventions, the pressures are not very different. The pleasures of companionship and shared enterprise are certainly the same. Newnham has always provided a place from which women can explore their intellectual and personal goals.

'Week nought' is packed with appointments and events. On Monday we meet to discuss the new students' first supervision with me. I give out reading lists, outline what is expected, and explain how to approach the task. Afterwards they seem optimistic and somewhat reassured; although one year I did have a student who announced at this point that she was going to go home and be a nurse (she didn't).

4th October

Both students and Fellows are formally admitted to the College on this day. It is a low-key but significant ceremony. Watching others sign the Newnham Register, I remember vividly the moment when I became a Fellow. I had no memory of signing as an undergraduate, presumably because of the fear afflicting me: the then College Secretary kindly found that earlier signature, to prove to me that I had not been an imposter for the preceding period of years.

5th October

Other welcomes follow. The College Feast is always a high point. Approaching from the dark gardens, the lights from Clough Hall have a fairytale quality. Inside, the hubbub is deafening, the Hall filled to capacity with Freshers in their new gowns, and the old hands in scarlet. The speeches often

Kennedy Hall.

draw on personal experience, and are invariably moving. I remember Mary Beard's inspirational talk at my own matriculation dinner, she having returned to Newnham, now as a Fellow, in that year. The message was (and remains) that with the strength of the Newnham community behind you, almost anything is possible, and you should reach for your dreams.

11th October
Term settles into a routine very rapidly. The timetable of lectures and supervisions requires discipline and stamina, but is great fun and extremely rewarding. It is a pleasure to see new students growing in confidence, and beginning to enjoy the extraordinary opportunities open to them. They are amazed to learn that once women could not attend lectures without the consent of the individual lecturers. Professors were paid by the University to give lectures open to any member of the University – a category which did not include women. There were also college lectures, usually more detailed and focused on Tripos, which were at first intended solely for the men in that particular college. It was recognised that this was not very efficient, and some lecturers began to admit students from other colleges. Henry Sidgwick was able to persuade several of these to admit women, also. Even if permission was forthcoming, the women had to be chaperoned, not just at the lectures themselves, but also when arriving and leaving. There were to be no encounters on staircases. The chaperones must have been quite adaptable, intellectually speaking. In 1878 Miss Clough is known to have accompanied Newnham students to lectures on Natural Sciences at Christ's, and on History at King's. She may well have been obliged to listen to other subjects elsewhere.

Miss Clough was described as 'a somewhat formidable person'. I suppose that some of us now might be similarly described. The level of contact with Senior Members is a privilege which current undergraduates come to appreciate, though they can find it a little daunting to be exposed to a level of individual scrutiny to which they are unaccustomed. Soon, though, the Freshers are learning to make the most of supervisions; contributing, questioning, and beginning to rely on themselves. Graduate students, also, are beginning to find their feet. They come from many intellectual and cultural backgrounds, and thus bring great interest and variety to College life. Although some Cambridge habits are puzzling to them, my overwhelming impression is of their desire to get stuck in to their work and to enjoy their surroundings to the full.

22nd October
Committee work is a significant commitment for the Vice-Principal during term. Newnham's comprehensive and inclusive committee structure is designed to ensure that all in the College can

Dr Catherine Seville giving a supervision.

contribute to every aspect of our governance, but not to waste time. The Governing Body (which all Fellows attend) meets twice this term, overseeing policy with a sharp eye. As might be expected, everyone has a view on everything, and discussions are constructive. Occasionally, an item proves unexpectedly controversial. The debate concerning the correct location for 'The Dolphin Boy' statue was the longest in my memory; but of course the gardens are rightly regarded as tremendously important. Much of the business of the College is handled by the Council, which usually meets fortnightly. Again, good sense and sound management are the characteristic qualities of these meetings, and always a positive attitude. There is good humour and a light touch in debate, also. Rumours that the Vice-Principal supported Red Nose Day by wearing one during a Council meeting cannot be denied, since the minutes confirm it.

Newnham is a sociable place. Senior Members regularly lunch together. Inevitably, a lot of business is done at the same time, but there is still time to enjoy the company of colleagues from all disciplines. Newcomers and guests often comment on the warm and welcoming atmosphere, and enjoy the laughter and conversation, particularly over coffee afterwards. For me, it is often a rejuvenating space in a crowded day. If the weather is good, a quick detour to take in the seasonal pleasures of the garden helps to clear the mind. The garden team is busy sweeping leaves at this time of year, and as the creeper starts to change colour from green to fiery red, the bright crisp sunshine brings out the best in the colour of the beautiful Champneys buildings. There are many marvellous events on offer, too; student concerts on Wednesdays, Pudding Seminars by members of the College on Fridays, the

Principal's Lodge Seminars (offering an eclectic and entertaining series of speakers), and a whole range of ad hoc talks of every description. All this helps to broaden and deepen the life of the College, and to cement links between its members.

28th November

Christmas approaches with a rush, and Music for the Festive Season usually falls at the very end of November. Clough Hall is beautifully decorated with a lovely tree, and there are Christmas Dinners every night of the last week of term, for those with the stamina. I see my undergraduates for end of term interviews, to discuss their supervision reports and to hear their own sense of their progress. The first years, in particular, are proud of what they have achieved in their first term, and now feel happily at home in Newnham. The snowmen (or perhaps women?) that pop up in the gardens are dressed wittily with Newnham scarves and carry empty bottles of wine.

29th November

The final week is heavy with committees, both in Newnham and in the Faculty, settling business for the end of the calendar year. Those of us on the Arts and Humanities Junior Research Fellowship Committee spend every spare minute reading a huge crop of applications. Competition is intense, and weighing candidates from one discipline against another is tricky, particularly since their research topics are hugely diverse. The successful candidate will be able to dedicate three years to her academic research, which is a rare privilege. These appointments are crucial in maintaining the flow of young academics, and Newnham is enriched by them.

6th December

Admissions interviews follow immediately after the end of term. This involves much complex coordination, since candidates will have at least two interviews, and may well have to sit a written test. Although the terrifying Cambridge Entrance and Scholarship Examinations have gone, it is still useful to see whether or not a candidate can write well to time. Particularly for those subjects which are not studied at A level, it is important to assess whether candidates can handle unfamiliar ways of thinking, or deal with material they have not prepared. For lawyers, speed, flexibility and the ability to look ahead are key qualities; as is a readiness to assess the interviewer's often challenging responses, and to adapt one's argument appropriately. Candidates tend to regard the

interviews with dread, but often enjoy the sparring far more than they expected to. Watching them begin to take pleasure in thought and argument can be a lot of fun for us all.

The interview process is far more controlled, structured, and transparent than it used to be. We are not permitted to ask about long journeys, unusual names, or what a candidate read on the train. Instead we are to confine ourselves to giving our name and subject, and outlining the structure, purpose and length of the interview. Interview reports are disclosed if requested, so it is no longer prudent to write, 'Face like a plate.' (a note that I saw on a Pool interview form in the 1980s). Although numbers of applicants now make this impossible, it used to be customary for the Principal to see each candidate. Dame Myra

Curtis (Principal 1942–54) pinned a brief note to the front of each file, presumably intended to encapsulate each candidate, to distinguish one from another after a long day of interviewing. 'Candidate T', for example, was described as: 'Dark, attractive looking – very vague (couldn't remember what her essay was about).' I have met several people who remember interviewing with Ruth Cohen (Principal 1954–72), who smoked a cigarillo, thereby shocking the more sheltered candidates. Candidates today would probably be equally taken aback if I did the same.

19th December

In the snowy days before Christmas I catch up with administration, and start on the backlog of academic work. My graduate students have produced outlines, drafts and chapters which need careful reading and assessment. I write a couple of book reviews, to publicise the work of colleagues in my field, and to help the editors of the relevant journals. My own research is on intellectual property, particularly copyright history. There is a query from the University Library, asking about the copyright status of various nineteenth-century publications of Swinburne's poetry, both in Britain and the United States. It is good to feel that my somewhat abstruse knowledge is of direct practical benefit to someone. I am also approached by a European radio station, asking if I will be interviewed about a proposed French law. Again, it is gratifying that people are interested! Christmas cards and messages arrive from former students all over the world, which is a delight. The Staff Christmas lunch, lively and relaxed, brings together all staff and Senior Members. It is a happy way to close a busy term.

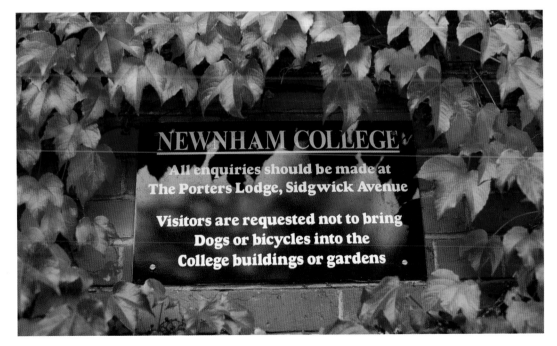

NEWNHAM COLLEGE

All enquiries should be made at
The Porters Lodge, Sidgwick Avenue

Visitors are requested not to bring
Dogs or bicycles into the
College buildings or gardens

Coming up

"My first day at Newnham, October 1962:

*A tiny, bare, cold room. My father photographed me
with our puppy, Susie, on the tiny bed. He'd bought me
a ragged gown at the Porters' Lodge for £2. He let Susie
out through the window to run around in the courtyard
of Sidgwick Hall. After they left I sat and cried. Later the
girl who had the room round the corner told everyone
'I looked out of my window and saw a hound of hell
rushing round the courtyard!' 'Susie's not a hound of
hell!' I protested, resentfully. Things did get better!"*

Lynne Armstrong (*Baldwin* NC 1962)

"I came up to Newnham in 1954, absolutely terrified, and cycling behind my luggage-filled taxi because I was afraid of getting lost. Immediately at home in Clough Hall, I met within the first hour a subsequently very good friend, and valued being surrounded by highly intelligent and interesting young women."

Gillian Hancock (NC 1954)

> On my first day, Principal Onora O'Neill addressed our nervous year of Freshers and told us that 'Newnham did not make mistakes; we were all supposed to be there'. Never have I felt more reassured."

Sally Singer (*Scott* **NC 1995**)

Freshers' meeting.

Matriculation

Newnham College Register Volume I: First student entry.

Above: Joan Bakewell (NC 1951).

> Once I was called up to sign the Register of the Roll my nerves changed to excitement. I felt a huge sense of pride but I was a bit worried that I'd smudge my signature and forever be remembered for my smudge and not my name."

Natasha D'Souza (NC 2009)

Matriculation, Clough Hall.

College (Newcomers') Feast

> *Dining in Hall below varnished portraits of our Founders, I remember thinking that one day I would know them. When I read Grace I sensed the weight of the privilege. Later, as my own books took me into Victorian times, the heritage became more familiar. Preparing a study of the fraudulent medium, Mrs Guppy, I was delighted to encounter Mrs Henry Sidgwick, earnestly investigating her. When in turn, we sink metaphorically beneath the lawns of Newnham, I like to imagine that we are all there, a congregation of women, from first to last.*"

Molly Whittington-Egan (*Tibbs* NC 1956)

'Cambridge Alumnae' Banner

The Banner was designed by Mary Lowndes and worked by students of Newnham and Girton. It was carried by the Cambridge contingent in the National Union of Women's Suffrage Societies' procession of 13 June 1908. On the banner the stencilled irises are for Newnham, the daisies for Girton.

This Banner has always resided in (and been cared for by) Newnham although arrangements have on occasion been made for it to be on show in Girton. It was displayed in the Senate House for the 1998 commemoration of the granting of degrees to women. As a stitched and stencilled textile it is a delicate artifact and is now displayed in a special case at Newnham which provides the necessary environmental protection.

Settling in

> *Arriving as a shy, gauche and nervous grammar-school girl, Newnham taught me to have confidence in myself and what I care about – and not to follow the crowd. The place and the people and my memories of my time there are totally intertwined: great teachers, tutors and friends, plus Newnham's supportive atmosphere, are pretty magical ingredients."*

Fiona Reynolds (NC 1976)

> *My parents were rather upset when, as they departed after delivering me to Newnham as a Fresher, I didn't wave or appear upset but immediately turned to join the friends I had already made in the few hours I had been there.*
>
> *Being able to make friends and mix with people who saw me as normal, after a lonely time as a clever child, gave me the confidence to be myself, and prepared me properly for adult life."*

Heather Coleman (NC 1984)

Below: Rosalind Franklin Building.

" *Living in one of Newnham's houses for graduates gave me the opportunity to meet students from round the world doing a wide range of courses. One of my enduring friends is an art historian. As a break from my intensive clinical medical course I would attend some of her lectures and visit museums with her.* "

Joanna M. Zakrzewska (NC 1977)

Left: Whitstead Graduate House.

Sidgwick Hall.

> I came from a background in the industrial north to this leafy paradise and its beauty overwhelmed me. And then it was the company I kept – really intelligent spirits – lively, curious and eager for life – the talk in Newnham was terrific."

Joan Bakewell (*Rowlands* NC 1951)

> What I enjoyed most about Newnham was making friends. We ate together every day, shared Ovaltine in our rooms, relaxed in the garden revising in May. We all had the same problems: essay crises, men, fitting in study amidst distractions of activities like music, politics, parties and punting. We could share our troubles but most of all we had a lot of fun."

Catherine Slater (*Malaiperuman* NC 1967)

1951.

Clough Hall.

Above: A 'coffin'.

Above: Bathroom, Kennedy Hall.

Students room. Newnham College. Cambridge

"The sparsely furnished room which could be personalised with posters.

The bureau and wooden storage box.

The welcome knock on the door interrupting essay writing.

The cold walk along the corridor to the baths, cleaned with rash-inducing scouring powder.

Tea in Clough Hall – doorsteps of wonderful fresh bread and jam."

Myfanwy Giddings (*Hughes* NC 1965)

Above: Senior Combination Room.

Left: The Newnham Twist Lamp, designed for the College to be free-standing or wall-mounted.

Right: Dadie Rylands' table: note the wine glass marks thought to have been left by members of the Bloomsbury Group.

a room of one's own

virginia woolf

Professor Mary Beard's room. Old Hall.

1941.

"*I remember that one of my joys was to have a coal fire in my room. We had plenty of coal in our own scuttles. I just loved lying in bed and watching the light from the flames playing on the ceiling.*"

Katharine Warrick (NC 1937)

"*On visiting Newnham recently I passed my third-year room and met the then occupant. We talked about the changes – a sink, wardrobe and internet link, but sadly no gas fire or gas ring. The curtains appeared unchanged. I was unfamiliar with gas when I arrived at Newnham, but enjoyed toasting crumpets for tea. One day I leaned towards the mirror above the fireplace just as I was about to go out and my long scarf swung onto the fire and caught alight!*"

Elizabeth Moyses (*Jessop* NC 1974)

"*I remember sitting beside the stained old bath tub in Clough, chatting to a friend who was washing herself and her clothes in the same water to save laundry … and pushing coins into the gas meter to make toast or use up milk by stirring in Bird's custard powder. All too frequently the custard boiled over, melting into the twisted cotton strands of the yellow hearthrug.*"

Caroline Johnson-Seiter (*Johnson* NC 1981)

Dr Liz Watson's room, Kennedy Hall.

> *Autumn 1954 started with a cold snap. To wit, the water in the cup on my windowsill froze. It was weeks before I learned to operate my gas fire sufficiently well to produce a flame more than half an inch high."*

Joan MacNaughton (*Ingold* NC 1954)

"For over fifty years I have thought of Newnham as one of the most visually satisfying buildings one could ever hope to live in. From any viewpoint, outside or in, the proportions are exactly right. The halls, the doorways, the staircases, the library entrance, the garden exits, windows, doorknobs and red-brick walls, all sit with their neighbouring piece of the structure in the most rational and friendly fashion. No part of the building sniffs at another: 'What on earth are **you** doing here?'"

Gillian Judd (*Graves* NC 1960)

"I lived in Peile for two years, in Eva Smith for another three, and so crossed Newnham's gardens every morning and evening. After dark, the atmosphere was peaceful, many windows were lit, sometimes the cats from the other side of the fence were still out and about; twice I even saw hedgehogs. During the day there were the trees and flowers and the red and white of the buildings to enjoy, the monument to sit down on, sunbathe and do your reading, the gardeners to chat to and learn from; and in the summer, there even were mulberries to eat. To this day, thinking of the gardens makes me happy."

Antonia Ruppel (NC 1998)

Strachey Building.

Peile Hall.

Looking towards Strachey.

Getting down to work

*You ask about supervisions. We have two a week, of an hour each, up in Miss Edmonds'
room. She has a very squashy sofa, and she sits in the middle, with one of us on each
side, and writes on an upturned tray!"*

Taken from a letter written to her parents by **Elizabeth Hartley (NC 1942)**

English seminar class being conducted by the Fellow in her home.

> *Newnham put me with world experts in my subject, allowing me the space to grow into a deep thinker, reader, critic and writer.*

Maggie Atkinson (*Cragg* NC 1975)

The Old Labs *c.*1910.

❝*We got arsenic and phosphorous fumes at the lecture yesterday morning and a frightful smell of ammonia in the Laboratory afterwards. It was perfectly disgusting. All the same chemistry is great fun and I did some splendid experiments.*❞

Catherine Holt (NC 1889)

Sports

> *Five bleary-eyed girls waiting for the cox to return with 'bow' who has overslept again. All wrapped up against the cold. Scarves wrapped like blankets over heads and necks. Still dopey from sleep but keen to get on the water. Aware that work done now could bring the glory of an 'oar' or even 'Head of the River'. NCBC could be burning a boat again at the Bumps supper."*

Roberta King (*Morris* NC 1981)

> *I will never forget that Newnham boosted my sense of self-worth and gave me the confidence to go out there and say 'Yes I can stand in front of ten million people and talk 'nonsense'!"*

Clare Balding (NC 1990)

1914–15.

The 'mixed' lacrosse team.

"*Misty mornings on the river, our coach silhouetted against the sunrise; anticipation as we returned to the Porters' Lodge and eyed our pigeonholes from afar; crew breakfasts in our socks in the Buttery (warm round rolls, butter and marmalade); notebooks by our doors stuffed with 'sorry I missed you' messages from people now too famous to remember us; ever-so-slightly sheepish men in the corridors; the Newnham banner unfurled for me on our wedding day.... tiny vignettes brim-full of memories.*"

Joanna Burch (NC 1983)

1919.

1923.

1941.

Tennis dress, 1889.

Opposite: Music for the Festive Season.

> *Freedom to explore, share and experiment in relaxed surroundings. We worked hard and enjoyed simple pleasures: marshmallows toasted on a coal fire, singing duets in adjacent baths, punting in summer and walking to Grantchester in winter.*
>
> *The long walk back to Peile, passing the Delphic Charioteer outside the Library; being caught cycling back to Newnham without a gown after an evening out."*

Mary Tredennick (NC 1952)

Opposite: Rosalind Franklin Building gate.

Newnham College. May 2011.

LENT TERM

Catherine's diary shows that for a Director of Studies, the New Year means the Pool.

4th January

The files of candidates who have just applied to Cambridge and missed a place at their first choice of College are assembled in Clough Hall. Crates of files are arranged by subject, on tables. It is normally very cold at first, but increasingly crowded and sociable. At busy times there is competition even to reach the boxes, let alone read the contents, and there is rarely anywhere to sit down. But there is always someone you know to talk to. The Pool is open for three days for consultation. On the final day there are subject meetings, attended by Directors of Studies, after which candidates may receive an offer or an interview from an interested college. The procedures are complex, but designed to achieve a fair process for candidates. It is a good way of smoothing out any bumpiness in application numbers, and of ensuring a consistent standard of entry across the Colleges.

17th January

Students are back in touch, asking for help with revision for mock examinations, and seeking references. Providing support for applications for courses and jobs is an important part of what Newnham offers. Directors of Studies' and Tutors' references are a part of this, but there are a host of other resources to tap into. The Associates have particularly useful pages on their website, and individuals are generous in their offers of both informal advice and formal placements. I am proud to say that the Law network is particularly vibrant. We hold biennial lunches, which all Law graduates and all those working in law-related fields are welcome to attend. Current Newnham Law students are placed with those who share their interests, at different stages in their lives and careers. Other subjects, too, hold Networking Lunches, with the same effect. More than anything explicit that Directors of Studies might say to their undergraduates, these gatherings of remarkable women bring it home to the students that their choices are wider than they perhaps have thought, and that their path ahead lies in their own hands. Encouragement and advice are far more valuable than they are costly.

25th January

The regular pattern of teaching and committees continues. The Library Committee, which I chair,

Opposite: The Pool. Clough Hall.

is one of my favourites. Newnham is privileged to have one of the best college libraries in Cambridge, thanks to the generosity of Henry and Elizabeth Yates Thompson. Comprehensively stocked, it is also a most beautiful and pleasant place to work in. The Yates Thompsons gave the College its original Library in 1897, and ten years later, the extension which nearly doubled the Library's capacity. At that time women were not permitted to use the University Library as of right. If a particular student was thought likely to make good use of the privilege, a special application could be made for a reader's ticket. However, even this concession was not, in practice, open to most women, because the Syndics enforced strictly a rule that readers had to be of age. Ella Bulley, one of the original five Newnham students, was granted a ticket in 1871, as she was already thirty years old. But many women were once more excluded, this time because they were too young. The inequity of these restrictions did, however, stimulate great generosity towards Newnham's library. We still enjoy those fruits today, and people's generosity continues. The beauty and convenience of the Yates Thompson Library has been appreciated by generations of Newnham students. Now connected to an airy and well-equipped modern extension, Newnham College Library continues to serve members of the College, and others. Our students still say that they love working in our library and know that they are lucky to have one of the best college libraries in Cambridge. Many will have favourite seats or preferred alcoves. Their affection is particularly apparent in the Easter term, when these hideaways are piled high with books, papers and revision notes.

7th February

Even in February, when crocuses are just peeping through the grass, we are beginning to think about the Examinations. Setting questions is painful work, although, naturally, the students have no sympathy for us. The challenge is to set a paper which allows a good student to show knowledge and ability, and permits an excellent candidate to excel. In Law papers (as in many other subjects), there are various hallowed traditions. Since the underlying legal matter might be considered rather dry, problem questions are likely to involve a whimsical and improbable set of facts, perhaps involving places and characters borrowed from a popular soap opera, their names only very thinly disguised. The effect of this 'humour' is somewhat limited by another custom. Within any question, no name may begin with the same letter, since the convention when writing the script is to shorten any reference to the person or place to the initial letter only. The papers go through a series of scrutiny processes, where both law and language are carefully checked by panels of examiners. I have had to amend questions to avoid the words 'Cinderella' (not necessarily known to international students) and 'grissini' (thought not to be a word generally known to students). Bonus points are awarded for a paper that goes through without correction. Although the tone of meetings is light, the underlying purpose is serious; papers must be clear, correct, and fair.

16th February

A relatively new tradition, Halfway Hall, offers a welcome break from these activities – a celebration of the mid-point of the students' undergraduate careers. Newnham's success in the Lent bumps

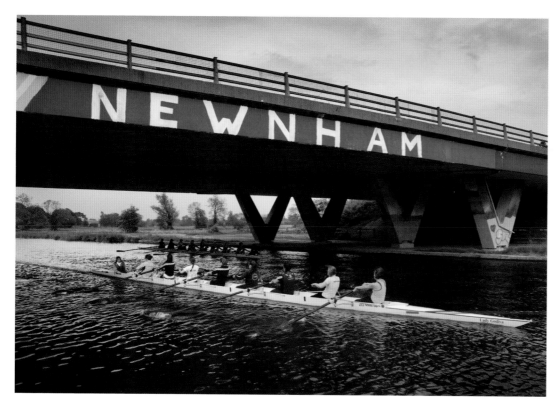

offers further cause for celebration, the daily results, as is traditional, are still chalked on a blackboard in the Porter's Lodge.

5th March

The Admissions Tutor asks me to speak to teachers at one of our regular open days, and to explain what we are looking for in a Law candidate. I am always glad to do this. Our approach is quite straightforward. We are interested in legal ability and motivation to study the subject, and these factors outweigh others (such as choice or number of A Levels). The teachers take the opportunity to ask many questions, and eventually seem reassured that there really is no trick to being offered a place. What counts is the inherent quality of their students.

12th March

As Term draws to a close, the focus for my students turns towards the task ahead. We discuss strategies for revision which will keep students thinking and

interested, rather than just cramming. As winter begins to ease a little, the more intrepid students take advantage of the occasional sunny days to eat their lunch in the garden.

9th April

Although the rhythm of life changes somewhat in the vacation, it is still busy. Sidgwick Hall buzzes with the voices of fifteen current students calling former students in our annual Telephone Campaign. They exchange news of Newnham today and learn from the alumnae what life was like here in the past. In the process they also hone their telephone interview skills and raise donations to support the College. There are two reunion events to look forward to. At Commemoration big tubs of daffodils outside the Porter's Lodge welcome alumnae and it is marvellous to see that those returning feel immediately and absolutely at home. I have heard many memorable speeches at Commemoration Dinner, though Miriam Margolyes' was unforgettable

– commencing with a characteristic account of her own time at Newnham, moving professionally through an irresistible exhortation to 'open our little handbags', and concluding with a most beautifully delivered joke. The urge to party in one's room does not seem to wear off with the passing of time. I was honoured to join one fiftieth anniversary class in Strachey. Someone had thoughtfully provided a bottle of whisky, which was being drunk from plastic tooth mugs. The conversation flowed. The MA Congregation is another pleasurable gathering and it is good to be able to focus on one particular year group. My own former students are now well-established in their first jobs, and keen to share news. One of them has just cycled from Lands End to John o'Groats – on a bicycle she was given by her peers when she was up at Newnham! I don't dare ask if she cycled down the corridor, but I expect so. They remark how much more fun it is to graduate without the strain of examinations. This reminds me of what lies ahead next term.

Literary archive launch

Above: Books by Newnham writers on display at the launch.

Opposite: Clockwise from far left:
Claire Tomalin (NC 1951); Sarah Dunant (NC 1969);
Eleanor Bron (NC 1957) and Nicola Beauman (NC 1963);
Katharine Whitehorn (NC 1947), Pam Hirsch, Karen Hodder
(NC 1960), Isabelle Anscombe (NC 1973), Miriam Margolyes
(NC 1960) and Janet Neel (NC 1959).

Pudding seminars

Lunchtime seminars given by students and Senior Members on their research – and every attendee gets a free pudding!

"Newnham had a huge impact on my life. Its warmth, vigour and inspirational teaching laid open a whole world of ideas and possibilities."

Julie Etchingham (NC 1988)

Associates' workshops

> *It is inspiring to meet our alumnae who have gone into successful careers in many different fields. I enjoy the talks and presentations, which are filled with practical advice, personal learning experiences, and a healthy dose of humour.*
>
> **Crystal Yeo (NC 2005)**

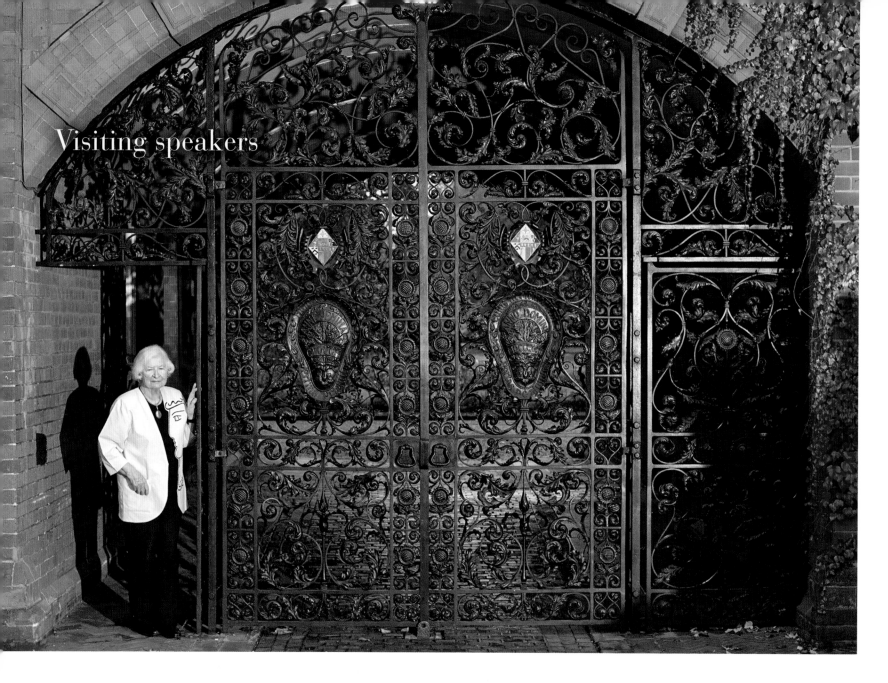

Visiting speakers

Griff Rhys Jones: *My secret life at Newnham.*

The Principal with Professor Dame Athene Donald, the speaker for the Henry Sidgwick Memorial Lecture: *Science – Awareness and Ignorance.*

P.D. James: *So you want to be a writer?*

Olivia Williams (NC 1986): *My career as an actress.*

Professor Mary Beard hosts students to meet Honorary Fellow and Classics scholar Professor Froma Zeitlin of Princeton University.

Library, archives and special collections

Rare books' room.

1941.

> *My special memory of Newnham is the smell and feel of the books as most of the rest of the College was slumbering. Somehow the authors I was reading seemed more immediately and intimately present when I was alone with them in the library at night.*

Celia Hawkesworth (*Williams* NC 1961)

Left: The Skilliter Centre for Ottoman Studies.

Below: The Archivist.

A selection of books by Newnham writers.

Halfway Hall

Special Formal Hall for second years marking the
mid-point between matriculation and graduation.

College governance and committees

The Governing Body.

The House Committee.

Domestic Bursary team meeting.

The College Council.

The Associates' Committee.

The Roll Committee.

The JCR Committee.

The MCR Committee.

The Campaign Board.

The Guild of Friends' Committee.

Reaching out to the future

Sixth Form Taster Day.

"Coming here has really opened my eyes and encouraged me to thoroughly think about applying here and that it's really achievable. I would like to apply here now as it would be an amazing place to study…. It was great because we got to control our own learning – when we found artifacts, we had to think about where they might have come from [and] why they were there…. Brilliant! The team made us feel like they cared what we had to say. Even though they were all practically genius [sic], they were refreshingly normal and friendly."

Comments from three sixth-formers who participated in the Archaeological Dig as part of Newnham's Outreach Programme.

Telephone campaign

Dress up night.

> *The telephone campaign is an opportunity to take a moment out of the hectic whirl of my present daily life, to reflect upon the path that brought me here and of course to indulge in some shameless nostalgia."*

Dawn Moody (NC 1986)

> *I was astounded by the generosity of the women I spoke with, the majority giving what they felt able to, all of which added up to a significant boost to Newnham.... stories of a wartime Cambridge hit by air raids and rationing were incredible. Yet I was struck by the fact that the Newnham they described was absolutely recognizable."*

Maddie Rea (NC 2007)

Commemoration

I found coming back to Commem immensely moving. Meeting women whom, in some cases, I had not seen for fifty years was very emotional. We all have our lives etched on our faces – some have had happy ones and some more difficult – and of course not all of us were there…. but once we started talking about what we have been doing, the same old personalities shone through and the years just disappeared – it was enormous fun."

Miriam Margolyes (NC 1960)

Newnham opened up my life. Orphaned at the age of three years, brought up by an aunt and uncle, my life had been very restricted, partly by the attitude of my guardians, partly by the war years. Newnham in 1946 was very exciting."

Evelyn Caulcott (NC 1946)

Rebellious and furious about the way Newnham College disciplined its students more strictly than the then all-male college treated their students, I did not appreciate the College at all when I was there…. Hindsight, however, makes me grateful that supervisions were enforced. I consider myself intensely lucky to have got a place in the days when women undergraduates were allotted only about one in ten of the Cambridge University places."

Celia Haddon (NC 1962)

Fiftieth anniversary reunion (1961).

*To walk in the footsteps of many great women
and the history they have paved on their
way, fighting prejudices to allow women
the right to an education, is something I am
immensely proud of. Newnham is defined by
its past, present and future. It is, in my view,
one of the most forward-thinking colleges in
Cambridge."*

Lizzy Cole (NC 2010)

101

Merchandise stall at Commemoration.

❝ Start of any blessing count is still that I got into Newnham. While cheerful, energetic and curious, I am not brilliant. My parents were intelligent but had no opportunity to study. Hove County Grammar School head Margaret Richards encouraged me to apply to Oxbridge. I learned from Ruth Cohen at interview that joining the Newnham community implied one belonged, and that all the support needed would be there. Accepting and being accepted by Newnham to read Natural Sciences (rejecting an offer from Oxford) revealed that I counted equal to anybody high or low, without the need to doubt or prove it, just the requirement to live life compassionately and to the full. ❞

Judy Moody-Stuart (*McLeary* NC 1960)

The Principal's Lodge.

Music and drama

At work in the gardens

1941.

The Garden Committee.

1941.

Peile Hall.

Kennedy Hall.

“ *I used to be able to slip quietly out of my beautiful wide ground-floor windows in Peile when the weather was fine and wander about in the garden for a while. Sometimes I would spot our agricultural economist Principal, Ruth Cohen, in the distance toiling mightily with her heavy-duty wheelbarrow – she loved that garden and dug in it. All this made Newnham's garden a garden with a difference – a garden to look up to – and perhaps one for which I have more respect than any other I have known since. It takes long-enduring communities to give communal gardens their special feel – and Newnham has had that from the very start. Newnham's garden has always been part of the heart-beating of the place.”*

Jo Elwyn-Jones (NC 1957)

EASTER TERM

EASTER TERM

As the business end of the year approaches the diary entries show the College gearing up to exams.

26th April

The first part of the Easter Term is very busy with teaching and marking. Students have extra supervisions to look over past papers, and lots of practice questions are written or planned. There is always a rush to submit dissertations by the due date, even though it is no secret that the University Regulations provide that they shall be submitted to the Secretary of the Faculty Board of Law no later than the seventh day of Full Easter Term. The deadline is noon. Inevitably, people's computers malfunction, and all the College's printers jam irremediably or run out of paper. The Law Faculty is hard hearted as regards all of these calamities. Examiners are instructed to deduct four marks if a dissertation is a day (or part of a day) late in submission, and two more marks per day thereafter. As one might expect from lawyers, when the rule was being drafted there was much discussion of hypothetical scenarios. What if, for instance, a student happened to be kidnapped on her way to the Faculty to deliver her dissertation? This was deemed a moot point.

20th May

The Henry Sidgwick Lecture, and the Dinner which follows, provide a welcome diversion from examination-related activities. It is one of our occasions at which 'Black Tie, Scarlet and Decorations' are worn, so the scene is very splendid. The days are lengthening, and often quite warm, so we can have drinks in the garden. The herbaceous borders are about to explode in an abundance of colour. Everyone wants to talk about the lecture, and to catch up with familiar faces or be introduced to new ones. In a reversal of the usual state of things, the revising students complain about the noise that we are making. A Porter is sent to admonish us. As High Table Steward and Wine Steward I have a particularly close interest in the dinner, since I have chosen the menu, and have been involved in buying the wine. Newnham's admirable catering staff understand how important shared meals are to the Newnham community, and have a finely tuned appreciation of the nature of the various events. As always, both food and wine are excellent, and guests seem at ease.

This is only a brief interlude from the main business of the term. Although many students are to be found lying on the lawns revising,

they are focused, and the atmosphere is tense. However, everyone is in the same boat, and there is also a sense of shared endeavour. Support and reassurance are always available, if needed. As an examiner, I am required to attend the first twenty minutes of the examination, in full academical dress. Some days there may be a visit from the Proctor, likewise resplendent. The custom is to bow, and doff caps (if worn). Our presence is not just an empty formality, but a sensible procedure which allows any problems or questions to be resolved quickly. It is very rare, but not unheard of, for the wrong version of the paper to be delivered, and the examiner is the person best placed to spot this. I must also check the candidates' statute books for illicit matter. The rules nowadays are very simple, in the interests of certainty and fairness. Permitted materials may not be marked in any way, other than with one's name and college on the inside front page. Tabs may be used, to allow navigation to landmark pages, but these must be transparent, so that nothing may be concealed beneath them. When I was a student there used to be fiendishly complicated rules regarding labelling, annotations, cross-referencing, circling and underlining, which no one seemed able to interpret with any certainty. They were glossed for me by my supervisor, who explained that one could do pretty much what seemed sensible, 'other than write one's notes in small on the inside front cover'. The boundaries of these restraints were not really relevant for me, though, since I lived in dread of taking a bus ticket in to the examination room accidentally and being ejected unceremoniously. I was quite put off in my own Land Law examination when the candidate in front of me was found to have unacceptable matter in the margins, and had his book taken

away. This is certain death in Land Law, given the technicalities of the subject.

Standing at the front of the examination room, one is struck by the particular quality of the silence. The candidates are intensely absorbed, minds working at top speed. I reflect on the fact that, for the first ten years of Newnham's history, women could not sit university examinations as of right. Nevertheless, some examiners were willing to allow their Tripos papers to be distributed to female students, and would mark them informally. Mary Paley, for example, was conspicuously successful in her studies, and took the Moral Sciences Tripos in 1874. All four examiners had to agree to let her take their examinations, and to mark her scripts. The examination papers were literally run from the Senate House to Professor Kennedy's house in Bateman Street. Professor Kennedy was the Regius Professor of Greek, and his daughter Marion Kennedy was Honorary Secretary to Newnham. The family's unwavering support for women's education, and the College, is commemorated by the naming of Kennedy Hall. It was not until 1881 that women were formally admitted to Tripos examinations. The names of the 'Class of female students' were listed separately, in order of merit, and the place that they would have occupied in the corresponding 'Class of Members of the University' was indicated. They received Tripos certificates rather than degrees. From 1921 women could be awarded titular degrees, and were admitted to instruction in the University (including the University Laboratories). But they remained excluded from the University Library, and from University government. Only in 1948 were women admitted to full membership of the University.

Professor Dame Alison Richard (NC 1966).

24th May

As soon as the students begin sitting their examinations, we start marking the scripts which emerge. They come to us, in distinctive red-stickered envelopes, via the Board of Examinations. We count them carefully, reconciling the bundles with our lists of what should be in them. A few candidates sit papers in their colleges, or in a computer suite, so stray scripts drift in late. The timetable is always tight, and the pressure is considerable. Scripts will be seen by at least two markers, and, since many of us will be marking several papers, there is the added difficulty of coordinating our marking schedules. Batches are exchanged by hand, for obvious reasons. Scripts are discussed. Marks are agreed. Mark books are checked and double checked. Examiners' meetings follow. These are often in May Week, so this does not offer the opportunity for relaxation and self-indulgence that might be imagined. Nevertheless, I still try to find time for the May Week Concert, and a glass of champagne on a lawn somewhere.

This year, one of the Junior Research Fellows was married in Newnham, which felt just right. May Week provides a perfect opportunity for students to celebrate and let their hair down after the examinations. The round of parties and activities is intense and exhausting. Each evening, excited Newnhamites in ball dresses are picked up from the Porters' Lodge by their partners, returning (often barefoot) in the early hours as the sun comes up. Newnham's June Event has become well known throughout the University. From my vantage point in the Pightle I have a good view of the queue stretching down Newnham Walk, as six hundred young people wait to be admitted through the Pfeiffer Arch. Once inside, they enjoy a wide variety of music, food and activities; blowing enormous bubbles, playing giant Jenga, watching the Chinese Dance Troupe or simply relaxing in the gardens. The MCR and Staff also celebrate with their own garden parties, at which jazz and the tempting smell of the barbecue offer distractions that examiners have to resist.

19th June

Once the examiners have made their determinations, the signed class-lists are delivered by hand to the Board of Examinations, for yet more checking. These are still posted outside the Senate House, in the traditional way. In addition, the results are simultaneously released by computer, allowing each student to learn her overall class in this more modern manner. The students are still keen to know their individual papers marks, though, so a queue still forms outside my door. Emotions on this day may be mixed; often delight or relief, but sometimes disappointment. It is a pleasure to see the successes, yet it may be hard to console the distressed. It is important to remember, though this may be very difficult at the time, that examination results are only a part of one's life at Newnham.

23rd June

Tonight we celebrate Newnhamites receiving two of the eight honorary degrees awarded by Cambridge this year: Alison Richard (NC 1966) and Mildred Dresselhaus (NC 1951).

Clough Hall.

2nd July

Graduation comes soon. The students panic about white blouses and purchase unsuitable shoes. They are delighted to be wearing academical dress – and rightly so. We assemble in the garden, outside Sidgwick Hall, where the rose beds near the sunken garden are in full bloom. Relatives and friends are dressed to the nines, and everyone is excited. The setting is quite beautiful, and it is easy to feel proud of one's students. The Praelector calls us to order, and the crocodile sets off through the Pfeiffer Arch. A battery of photographers surrounds us, and the intrepid stand on walls and even bollards to capture the perfect shot. It is fun to be so much the focus of public attention, particularly when the cars stop to let us walk through the traffic lights at the bottom of Sidgwick Avenue. The Head Gardener goes ahead to ensure that no driver is foolish enough to consider anything but pulling over. In the Senate House, there is much ceremony, and an array of gorgeous official attire. It is a dignified occasion, and an important one for each graduand. A group of us wait outside, at the Doctor's door in Senate House passage. The new graduates emerge, blinking in the light, to well deserved congratulation. More photographs follow, on the Senate House lawn. Before the walk back to Newnham, a quick coffee may be necessary, or, on a hot day, an ice cream. The buffet for the graduands and their guests is one of the most enjoyable events of the year. The gardens look stunning, and we are usually lucky with the weather. People spread out all over the lawns, and enjoy their picnic and strawberries. I love to meet my students' families, and am touched by their warmth. I seem to be a familiar figure to them, even if we have not actually met. Graduation is a significant rite of passage for each graduand, and it is a great pleasure to see them launched on a new phase of life.

8th July

One more week of committees follows for us. The Education Committee offers a valuable opportunity to share not just successes and disappointments, but also ideas and strategies. We award a satisfying number of prizes and scholarships, too. There is a similar meeting to award graduate studentships and prizes. It is hugely important to support young academics at this early stage of their careers. We see from their proposals that the range and quality of their work is impressive.

That night we hold the Leavers' Party, always a special evening of fellowship, which marks the unofficial end to the Senior Members' academic year. The Long Vacation Term (or, the Research Period, as it is officially known) has begun. Throughout July I teach on a course in the Law Faculty, introducing foreign lawyers to the common law system. I am glad to have time to turn to my research again, also. August is very quiet – at least until the A-level results come out, and the cycle of the academic year restarts. Once again, I look forward to meeting my new students, and to the return of the current students. In this coming year at Newnham, their hopes, ambitions and potential will be nurtured and developed – as so many students have found in the previous hundred and forty years.

In writing this piece I have consulted a number of works, including: Alice Gardner, *A short history of Newnham College Cambridge* (Cambridge: Bowes & Bowes, 1921); Mary Agnes Hamilton, *Newnham, an informal biography* (London, Faber and Faber, 1936); Ann Phillips (ed.), *A Newnham Anthology* (Cambridge: Newnham College 1979); Gillian Sutherland, *Faith, Duty and the Power of Mind* (Cambridge: Cambridge University Press, 2006); Rita McWilliams Tullberg, *Women at Cambridge* (Cambridge: Cambridge University Press, 1998).

Revision and exams

> During Finals, I turned on an electric fire, and returned from collecting my post to find my room (and revision notes) ablaze. Thankfully no one was hurt, and the Cambridge fire brigade had a field day. I wrote to my Tutor Ann Philips asking to see her, and fearfully presented myself. 'Oh thank goodness', she said briskly, when I explained my room was totally destroyed. 'When I got your note I was worried you were in trouble. So how are the exams going?' I moved in with my Trinity boyfriend and got a 2:1, without the notes. "

Sue Delafons (NC 1977)

" *I remember worrying about how on earth I was going to condense all that I had learned into three hours' worth of writing.*"

Dorothy Henderson (NC 1979)

CORRIDOR CLOSED

EXAMS IN PROGRESS

1941.

127

Behind the scenes

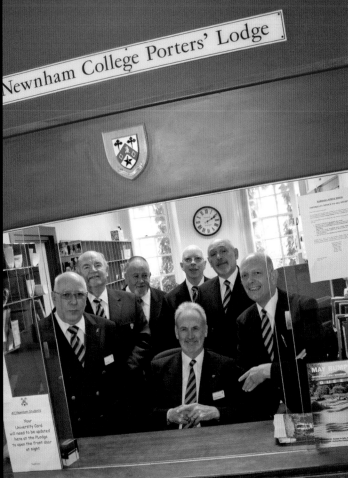

Newnham College Porters' Lodge

Housekeeping.

Development.

Gardeners.

Domestic Bursar and Head Housekeeper.

Bursary.

Principal's team.

Admissions.

I'll never forget my interview at Newnham – I had 'auditioned' for a college in Oxford with two gentlemen whose faces had curdled with disapprobation when I'd expressed an interest in the performing arts and I was not expecting much. After an afternoon with Jean Gooder and Sita Narasimhan, I was walking on air – the sense of being heard, truly understood and then nudged into clarification was overwhelming. I'm afraid I stole an IN/OUT tray to celebrate my high for which I got a row from my parents. They then nailed it to the back of the front door. I'll always be grateful to Newnham and its extraordinary teaching. I'll always feel slightly guilty about that IN/OUT tray."

Emma Thompson (NC 1978)

FIRST FLOOR

GROUND FLOOR

May Week

> *Fritillaries in the gardens and collecting armfuls of Queen Anne Lace for the vase on my mantelpiece. Knowing that someone had their kettle on when my lights dimmed – an opportunity for a chat on poetry, history, ethics or men! Newnham is the very antithesis of ivory towers – we could walk on the grass and dance down the corridors with girls from London council estates and princesses from Malaysia. 'My heart leaps up when I behold....': Wordsworth's words not mine, but they sum up what Newnham means to me."*

Deepa Parry-Gupta (*Gupta* NC 1987)

Graduation

Rehearsal.

> *I graduated at the Senate House in 1949, which was the first year that women were included in this ceremony. I nearly missed this occasion because the gown I had reserved was not available and so I asked a bystander who had just graduated to lend me his gown, which he very kindly did.*

Janet Riddlestone (*Warham* NC 1946)

Graduation 2010.

Graduation 2011.

" *Truly the alumnae of Newnham College are a formidable and remarkable group of women.* "

Professor Dame Alison Richard (NC 1966)
former Vice Chancellor University of Cambridge

List of Subscribers

This book has been made possible through the generosity of the following subscribers.

Dates indicate year of matriculation.

Anita R Abrams (*Berlyne* NC 1947)
Hester Abrams (Mrs Wax) (NC 1982)
Rachel Abrams (NC 1992)
Rebecca Abrams (NC 1982)
Susan Abrams (Mrs Reizenstein) (NC 1974)
Janice Adams (*Woor* NC 1964)
Josephine Adams (NC 1978)
Lydia Aers (NC 1996)
Myriam Nathalie Ahmed (NC 2007)
Natasha Ahmed (NC 2002)
Anna Pilar Ainslie (NC 2009)
Rabia Ilay Akbulut (*Peerzada* NC 2009)
Dr Julia Aked (NC 1983)
Michelle Viteri Alarcón (NC 2005)
Gemma-Claire Ali (NC 2009)
Karina Ali-Noor (NC 2005)
Jessie Allen-Williams (*Findley* NC 1943)
Mrs E C Allison (NC 1952)
Christabel Ames-Lewis (*Keith-Roach* NC 1959)
Katharine Ames-Lewis (NC 1964)
Nor Hidayah Binte Mohd Amin (NC 2010)
Ms Rolande Anderson (NC 1973)
Sophia Anderson (NC 2009)
Rosemary Andreae (*Gilbert* NC 1967)
Lucy Andrews (NC 2007)
Caroline Crews Angle (NC 2009)
J Mary Appleyard (*Maurer* NC 1968)
Professor Elizabeth Archibald (NC 1969)
Sarah Armstrong (*Buckley* NC 1981)
Natalie Arrowsmith (NC 2007)
Diana Arundale (*Kew* NC 1954)
Diane Ashby (*Wheeldon* NC 1980)
Anne Elizabeth Ashford (NC 1962)
Anna Ashton (*Rylander* NC 1952)
Rachael Ashton (NC 2007)
Mary Ashworth (NC 1943)
Dr Hazel Assender (NC 1987)
Dr Maggie Atkinson (*Cragg* NC 1975)
Alison Attfield (*Jones* NC 1977)
Christine Ayton (*Macleod* NC 1977)
Claire S Badgery (NC 2006)
Julia M Bailey (NC 2010)
Dr Mary Baines (NC 1951)
Dr Cecilia Bainton (*Elliott* NC 1973)
Joyce Baird (NC 1948)
Sarah Baird (*Le Page* NC 1979)
Joan Bakewell (NC 1951)
Harriet Balcombe (*Stack* NC 1981)
Francesca Balestrieri (NC 2009)
Alexandra Barker (*Millward* NC 2002)
Dr Claire Y Barlow
Dr Sylvia Barnard (NC 1959)
Katy Barnes (NC 1998)

Pauline Barnes (NC 1970)
Joan Barraclough (*Ronald* NC 1952)
Dr Carolyn C Barshay-Szmidt (*Szmidt* NC 1995)
Nicola Louise Bartley (*Caffrey* NC 1993)
Flora Barton (NC 2007)
S C Bartram and Family (NC 2009)
Sylvia Baylis (NC 1977)
Jane Bell (*Seaman* NC 1966)
Kathy Benham (*Bradbury* NC 1978)
Sheila M Bennett (NC 1981)
Crista Benskin (NC 1979)
Rachael Benson (NC 2010)
Karin-Elin Berg (NC 1997)
Helen Berry (NC 1990)
Katie Bewlock (NC 2010)
Jane Biddell (NC 1976)
Rosalie Bidgood (*Dunlop* NC 1970)
Helen Billington (NC 1979)
Laura Birkinshaw-Miller (NC 2008)
Hilary H Birks (*Lees* NC 1962)
Jennifer Bisset (NC 1981)
Jocelyn Blackburn (NC 1953)
Gillian Blake (NC 2008)
Katharine Blake (NC 1951)
Susan Blake (NC 1971)
Shirley Booth Blancke (NC 1954)
Rachel Blight (NC 1998)
Sarah Blomfield (*Hartley* NC 1990)
Ailsa Bloomer (NC 2008)
Dr Fiona Eve Blumfield (*Yoffey* NC 1971)
Mrs E M Blyth (NC 1945)
Jenny A Body (*Tindill* NC 1964)
Anne Bolton (NC 1976)
Mary Bolton (NC 1984)
Gill Booth (*Harvey* NC 1965)
Sarah Bostock (*Parker* NC 1991)
Janet Boswood (*Martin* NC 1955)
Rachel Boulton (*Gresford Jones* NC 1957)
Mrs Gill Brackenbury (*Huddart* NC 1982)
Maureen Bragg (NC 1946)
Leah Bramwell (NC 2008)
Catherine Breheny (NC 1989)
Dr Barbara Brend (NC 1959)
Dr June E Brett (NC 1946)
Anna Brewin (NC 2008)
Angela Bridges (*Collinson* NC 1974)
Maxine Alison Briggs (NC 1987)
Felicia Emma Britton (NC 2010)
Alison Evelyn Snodgrass Bromhead (NC 1969)
Jilyan Bromley (*Kelly* NC 1982)
Jennifer Brotherton (NC 1960)
Alison Luford Brown (NC 1974)
Belinda Brown (NC 1948)

Carole Brown (NC 1988)
Emma L Brown (NC 2008)
Lisa Brown (NC 1999)
Ann Brumfit (*Sandars* NC 1958)
Amber V L Bryan (NC 1999)
Susan Elisabeth Bryce (*Balkwill* NC 1949)
Anne Frances Bullock (*Smith* NC 1976)
Sarah Alexandra Bunn (NC 1995)
Yajai Bunnag (NC 2006)
Margaret Bunt (*Dance* NC 1946)
Dr Joanna Burch (NC 1983)
Gail Burn (*Metcalf* NC 1980)
Alice Burnett (NC 1991)
Laura Burnett (NC 1995)
Rebecca Burrell (NC 2005)
Dr Sophie Cabral (NC 1986)
Jackie P Cain (NC 1980)
Alice Cairns (NC 2007)
Sophie Cameron (NC 1990)
Emma Louise Camilleri (NC 2010)
Margaret Campbell (NC 1966)
Elizabeth R A Campion (NC 2010)
Christine A P Canham (*Jones* NC 1960)
Philippa Carbutt (NC 1991)
Gwyneth Card (NC 2001)
Carol Carlisle (*Hutt* NC 1947)
Catherine Caro (NC 1991)
Christina F Carr (NC 1978)
Mary A Cascio (NC 1974)
Dr Edwina Casebow (NC 1999)
Claudia Catacchio (NC 2004)
Mrs Evelyn Caulcott (NC 1946)
Janet A Ceasar (NC 1953)
Andrea C Cervi (NC 1976)
Danielle Lucy Champion (NC 1997)
Carmen Chan (NC 1991)
Rachel Seen Yin Chan (NC 2008)
Wendy Hiu-Ying Chan (NC 1993)
Deborah Chancellor (*Mowbray* NC 1985)
Alison Chapman (NC 1978)
Emma Rosamund Chapman (NC 2009)
Jill Booty Chapman (NC 1953)
Isabel Charles (NC 1972)
Dr R Charles (NC 1987)
Shirley Ann Charters (NC 1952)
Xi Chen (NC 2002)
Erica Anne Chessman (NC 1996)
Susan C Chester (*Darling* NC 1969)
Liz Chidley (NC 1970)
Rachel Christophers (*Williams* NC 1952)
Selene Chua (NC 1982)
Yousun Chung (NC 2008)
Fiona Clark (*Dziegiel* NC 1981)

Anne Clarke (*Pudsey-Dawson* NC 1980)
Jane Clarke (*Vangen* NC 1985)
Stephanie Frances Clemens (NC 2000)
Hannah Clemo (NC 2007)
Dame Julia Cleverdon (NC 1969)
Julia Coates (*Clarke* NC 1985)
Sarah Cobb (*Pryor* NC 1979)
Jan Cobley (*Lowe* NC 1969)
Dr Claire Elizabeth Cockcroft (NC 1994)
Linda Coe (NC 1975)
Penelope Coggill (*Bailey* NC 1968)
Elizabeth Coker (NC 2008)
Lizzy Cole (NC 2008)
Emma Elizabeth Coleman (NC 1989)
Heather Coleman (NC 1984)
Suzanne Coles (NC 1990)
Melanie Collier (NC 1995)
Jane Collins (*Rees* NC 1962)
Rebecca Louise Collins (NC 2006)
Emily Coltman (*Baker* NC 1995)
S M Colwell (NC 1970)
Laura Comber (NC 1996)
Melanie Comer (NC 1983)
Mrs Frances Cook (*Binney* NC 1965)
Sheila Cook (NC 1943)
Dr Felicity Cooke (NC 1981)
Jane Cooper (*Westwood* NC 1958)
Mrs Mithoo Nadirshah Coorlawala (*Chenoy* NC 1938)
Elizabeth Ann Corbett (NC 1989)
Alison Cork (NC 1982)
Alison Coupe (*Campbell* NC 1988)
Elizabeth Coupe (NC 1986)
Jackie Cove-Smith (Dr J M Morgan) (NC 1961)
Eleanor Cowie (NC 1961)
Sarah Craig (*Gowlett* NC 1987)
Yvonne Craig (*Inskip* NC 1955)
Ophelia Crawford (NC 2010)
Sara Croll (NC 2007)
Effie Crompton (NC 1955)
Emma Cross (NC 2006)
Mrs Sara Crouch (*Pennington* NC 1982)
Joanna Crowe (NC 1972)
June Crown (*Downes* NC 1956)
Rose Croxford (NC 1982)
Gill Cruickshank (*Riches* NC 1954)
Jan Cuff (*Craze* NC 1963)
Joan Cull (*Ross* NC 1952)
Kirsten Cummins (NC 1989)
Lesley Cundiff (*Secker* NC 1977)
Lucy Elinor Cundliffe (NC 2002)
Josephine Cundy (*Boyd* NC 1964)
Jane Louise Elizabeth Curry (*Finch* NC 1972)

Claire Curtis (NC 2001)
Mrs Rosamund Curtis
Julia Jennifer D'Arcy (NC 2005)
Amanda Dalcassian (NC 1982)
Barbara Dalton (NC 1946)
Jane Dalton Holmes (*Williamson* NC 1959)
Jane Dancer (NC 1981)
Emma Danks (NC 1993)
Kate Davenport (*Hackett* NC 1976)
Alexandra Davies (NC 2008)
Anne Davies (*Gracey* NC 1973)
Charlotte A Davies (NC 2010)
Mrs Elizabeth Davies (*Stewart* NC 1993)
Jayne Davies (*Whyman* NC 1976)
Ursula Davis (NC 1951)
Lucy J Davison (NC 1991)
Dilys Daws (*Kahn* NC 1954)
Rebecca Dawson (NC 1997)
Angélique Day (NC 1973)
Jill Day (NC 1953)
Sue Delafons (NC 1977)
Dr Carol Deller (Mrs Pocock) (NC 1956)
Marcus Delph
Yandi Deng (NC 2008)
Sabrina Derham (NC 2008)
Amanda Derrick (*Barton* NC 1974)
Vivienne Dews (NC 1971)
Katharine Louise Dexter (NC 1986)
Gabriela Dhir (NC 1998)
Jean Dibben (*Turnock* NC 1955)
Rosemary Dickin (NC 2004)
Wiebke Bettina Dietrich (NC 2000)
Jennifer Dines (NC 1957)
Lindsay Dobson (*Rylatt* NC 1990)
Belinda Dodd (NC 1983)
Dr Louise Dolan (NC 1979)
Alison Donnithorne-Tait (NC 1972)
Sharon Dooley (NC 1995)
Janet Doran (*Stevens* NC 1968)
Alison Doubleday (NC 1960)
Margaret Dougherty (*Waghorn* NC 1955)
Caroline Drake (*Boalch* NC 1982)
Sara Drake (NC 1975)
Sophie Drummond (NC 2009)
Dr Kirsten Duckitt (Mrs Cannatella) (NC 1983)
Claire Dudley (NC 2001)
Miriam Dudley (NC 1977)
Anne Duncumb (*Taylor* NC 1950)
Dr Philippa Dyson (*Howard* NC 1940)
Jo Eames (NC 1983)
Sarah Earl (NC 2010)
Professor Pat Easterling (NC 1952)
Susan Eden (*Rees* NC 1961)
Anne Maria Egan (NC 1977)
Jane Eimermann (NC 1984)
Anne E Eldred (*Taylor* NC 1976)
Wendy Ellicock (NC 1968)
Amanda Elmes (*Green* NC 1992)
Katie Emslie (NC 1996)
Nazli Eralp (NC 2009)
Juliet Evans (*Wilson* NC 1968)
Wendy Evans
Coralie Evison (*Evans* NC 1990)

Laura Jane Eyre (NC 2005)
Josephine Falk (NC 1963)
Julia Gabriele Athina Faltermeier (NC 2009)
Yucy Fang (NC 2007)
Mrs H K E P Farnsworth (*Remy* NC 1952)
Penelope Farquhar-Oliver (*Keddie* NC 1961)
Claire Fellows (*Armstrong* NC 1990)
Mrs Valerie Fenwick (NC 1956)
Laura Fergus (NC 2010)
Dr Jane Ferguson (NC 1981)
Elizabeth Anne Fieldhouse (*Cross* NC 1996)
Asma Fikree (NC 1996)
Luisa Filby (NC 2010)
Kirsty Nichol Findlay (NC 1965)
Marie Finnis (*McNally* NC 1962)
Dr Helen Firth
Anne Fletcher (NC 1977)
Kerrie Fletcher (NC 1991)
Andrea Florence (NC 1978)
Dr Gillian Flower (*Smith* NC 1962)
Susan M Flynn (*Greig* NC 1966)
Margaret de Fonblanque (*Prest* NC 1963)
Jess Ford (NC 2008)
Jane Fordham (NC 2004)
Louise Forte (*Dalby* NC 1962)
Dr Valerie Fowler-Hungerford (NC 1971)
Margaret Frampton (*Jones* NC 1952)
Sylvia Freedman (*Zeffert* NC 1954)
Dr Jane Freeston (NC 1995)
Dr Elizabeth French (NC 1949)
Sarah Frost (*Lee* NC 1990)
Natalie Fullwood (NC 2001)
Linda Fussey (*Skewes* NC 1965)
Dr Catarina Gadelha
Mary Galbraith (NC 1954)
Marion Gale (NC 2008)
Pamela Gale (*Green* NC 1951)
Jenny Garland (NC 1971)
Kori Lee Garner (NC 1977)
Amelia Medina Rose Garnett (NC 2008)
Zalyah Gazali (NC 2010)
Debjani Ghosh (NC 1998)
Katherine Gibbs (NC 2008)
Louise Gibbs (*Dickson* NC 1982)
Myfanwy Giddings (*Hughes* NC 1965)
Dr Jean Giess (*Tunnicliffe* NC 1974)
Olivia M G Gillespie (NC 1991)
Seánin Gilmore (NC 1991)
Josephine Gladstone (*Elwyn-Jones* NC 1957)
Mary Gladstone (NC 1943)
Mrs Patsy Glazebrook College Nurse
Karen Gledhill (NC 1979)
Sara Elizabeth Gledhill (NC 1983)
Alison Glen (*McIntosh* NC 1982)
Liz Gloyn (NC 2001)
Shabana Glynn (NC 1983)
Bettina M M Göbels (NC 2002)
Helen B Goddard (*Ross* NC 1965)
Ann Godfrey (*Baker* NC 1960)
Mrs Shelagh Godwin (NC 1966)
Beatrice Goldie (NC 1955)
Caroline M H Goodall (NC 1974)
Pat Goode (*Smeed* NC 1947)

Jean Gooder
Janet Goodman (NC 1972)
Jean Goose (NC 1957)
Margaret Goose (NC 1964)
Alashiya Gordes (NC 2007)
Rachel Gordon (NC 2010)
Gillian Goss (*Page* NC 1954)
Diana S Gould (NC 1944)
Anna Goulding (NC 2007)
Betty, Lady Grantchester (NC 1943)
Eleanor Great (NC 1987)
Coryn Greatorex-Bell (NC 1971)
Sally Greaves (*Doherty* NC 1966)
Jenifer Green (*Proctor* NC 1950)
Dr Celia Greenberg (*Prynne* NC 1966)
Virginia Greenburgh (NC 1948)
Joen Greenwood (NC 1961)
Ruth E Greenwood (NC 1979)
Lindsay Greer (NC 1969)
Maggie Gregory (*Fletcher* NC 1968)
Martha Grekos (NC 2000)
Oenone Grice (*Bean* NC 1984)
Emma Griffiths (NC 2009)
Dr Yvonne Griffiths (*Humphreys* NC 1952)
Judith Grimditch (NC 1959)
Mrs Daphne Groat (*Butterwick* NC 1958)
Janet Gruber (NC 1976)
Dr Hilary S D Gunkel (*Smith* NC 1965)
Anna Gurevich (NC 2010)
Jean Guy (*Aldridge* NC 1960)
Lene Haagensen (NC 1993)
Karen Habermann (NC 2009)
Sarah K Hack (NC 2009)
Clare Hadley (NC 1977)
Diane M Haigh (NC 1968)
Alexandra Haining (*White* NC 1979)
Elisa Haining (NC 2007)
Charlotte Halkett (*Nolan* NC 1997)
Ann Hall (*Stickland* NC 1956)
Dr Kay Hall (*Harper* NC 1978)
Lucy C Hall (*Anderson* NC 1952)
Sarah Ann Hall (NC 1984)
Victoria Hall (NC 2008)
Gillian Halliday (NC 1975)
Judith Halnan (*Allison* NC 1953)
Dr Heidi M Hamer (NC 1983)
Elizabeth Hamilton (*Driver* NC 1973)
France Hamilton (*Millet* NC 1966)
Clare Hamon (NC 1974)
Gillian Hancock (NC 1954)
Valerie J Harland (*Platt* NC 1950)
Kim Harmer (NC 1989)
Briony Harrison (*Chui* NC 1992)
Dr Diane Hatton (NC 1984)
Celia Hawkesworth (NC 1961)
Clare Hawley (NC 1986)
Joanna Hawthorne Amick (NC 1975)
Gillian Haydon (*Hand* NC 1982)
Frances Hazlehurst
Heather Head (*Otridge* NC 1972)
Joan K Heath (NC 1974)
Mary Heathcote (NC 1978)
Deborah Hedgecock (NC 1987)

Jo Hedley (NC 1984)
Angela Heeley (*Tyrrell* NC 1997)
Margaret Helmore (*Martin* NC 1947)
Dorothy Henderson (NC 1979)
Dr Isabel Henderson (NC 1955)
Bridget Ann Henisch (*Wilsher* NC 1950)
Malithi Sumali Hennayake (NC 2009)
Barbara Hennings (NC 1976)
Inal Henry (NC 2002)
Eileen Hepworth (*Gillibrand* NC 1982)
Katherine Herzberg (NC 1965)
Judith Herzig (*Robinson* NC 1959)
Judy Herzmark (*Dobbs* NC 1946)
Anne Hewitt (NC 1975)
Rt Hon. Patricia Hewitt (NC 1967)
Anthea Heyes (NC 2006)
Tessa Hicks (*Wolferstan* NC 1976)
Dr Emma Higham (*Chadwick* NC 1989)
Emily Hirst (NC 1997)
Lydia Hirst (*Pesate* NC 1976)
Bridget Hobson (*Main* NC 1976)
Deborah Hodder
Karen Hodder (NC 1960)
Patricia Hodgson (NC 1965)
Suzanne Hodgson (NC 1966)
Ann R Holden (NC 1974)
Kerry A Holder (NC 1988)
Joan Holgate (NC 1946)
Dr Meridel Holland (NC 1965)
Linda Holmes (Alexander) (NC 1983)
Patricia Hing Tong Hon (NC 1985)
Jo Honigmann (NC 1988)
Caroline Hope (*Bush* NC 1965)
Mrs M O Horrell (NC 1953)
Yasmin Hosain (*Safdar* NC 1957)
Claire Jean Hou (NC 2007)
Becky House (NC 2010)
Gill Houston (NC 1980)
Nicola Houston (NC 1993)
Mei Yin How (NC 2005)
Margaret Howe (*Mence* NC 1943)
Virginia J Howe (*Frith* NC 1946)
Laura Howell (NC 2009)
Jun Huang (NC 2005)
Penelope Hubbard (NC 1979)
Rebecca Ann Hughes (NC 2010)
Aoife Hulme (*Mulhall* NC 1999)
Valerie Humphreys (*Williams* NC 1954)
D Margaret Hunt (*Jenkins* NC 1966)
Victoria Hunter (*Manby* NC 1996)
Jacqui Huntley (*Paice* NC 1968)
Rebecca Hutchinson (NC 2004)
Claire Hutchison (NC 1988)
Dr Amanda Hynes (NC 1992)
Ruth Hannah Robin Innes (NC 2007)
Alice Insley (NC 2008)
Linda M Intelmann (NC 2010)
Camilla Elizabeth St Aubyn Jackson (NC 2009)
Sonia Jackson (*Edelman* NC 1953)
Anne Jacobsen (NC 1946)
Helen Jameson (NC 1977)
Christine Janis (NC 1970)
Valerie Jaques (NC 1961)

Dr Zahra Jawad	(NC 2000)
Mihiri Jayaweera	(NC 1985)
Patricia Jeffery	(*Chambers* NC 1965)
Hilary Jeffreys	(*Bates* NC 1944)
Lesley Jenkins	(*Haines* NC 1967)
Melissa Jennings	(NC 1988)
Victoria Jennings	(NC 1995)
Ursula Jepson	(*Taylor* NC 1941)
Elizabeth Mary Jewell	(NC 1950)
Brenda F O Jillard	(NC 1951)
Alison M Johnson	(NC 1960)
Elizabeth G Johnson	(NC 1980)
Gwyneth Johnson	(*Bateman* NC 1959)
Mrs Pat Johnson	(*Armstrong* NC 1956)
Caroline Johnson-Seiter	(NC 1981)
Amanda Jane Jones	(*Corry* NC 1966)
Clare Jones	(*Strong* NC 1989)
Deborah Jones	(*Bayfield* NC 1980)
Hannah Elizabeth Jones	(NC 2008)
Joyce Rosemary Jones	(*Adams* NC 1973)
Liz Jones	(NC 1999)
Veena Joory	(NC 1997)
Saskia Jordan	(*Baguley* NC 1987)
Rebecca Joseph	(NC 2007)
Gillian Judd	(*Graves* NC 1960)
Dr Tanya Kamchamnong	(NC 1994)
Satoko Kametaka	(NC 2009)
Joanna Katsiolidou	(NC 2009)
Kate Kelly	(*Gurney* NC 1982)
Catherine Emma Kennedy	(NC 1988)
Shan Kennedy	(NC 1976)
Rachel Kenny	(*Thomson* NC 1986)
Susan Kew	(*Steele* NC 1973)
Parisut Kimkool	(NC 2009)
Victoria Kimonides	(NC 1993)
Julia King	(NC 1977)
Marion Kinns	(*Tomkys* NC 1964)
Sue Kistruck	(*Waterfield* NC 1955)
Hannah Louise Kitchener	(NC 2006)
Joanna Kitchin	(NC 1946)
Sarah-Jane Kitching	(NC 1981)
Frances M G Klein	(*Platt* NC 1961)
Riamsara Kuyakanon Knapp	(NC 2010)
Margaret Knott	(NC 1932)
Vasiliki Kokkalidou	(NC 2007)
Angelyn Konugres Coupounas	(NC 1956)
Tania Nadia Kossberg	(NC 2007)
Bosiljka Kozomara	(NC 2009)
Sally Kynan	(NC 1971)
Amandeep (Ams) Lafferty	(*Samra* NC 2001)
Mary Lambell	(NC 1957)
Caroline Lamont Smith	(NC 1994)
Bella Lamplough Shields	(NC 2010)
Dr Pamela Stent Langlois	(NC 1958)
Claire Lannon	(NC 1989)
Amy Pui Shan Lau	(NC 1992)
Sarah Laville	(*Ferguson* NC 1986)
Rosemary Lawless	(NC 1986)
Sophie Lawrance	(*Strong* NC 1992)
Caroline A Lee	(NC 1998)
Jaime Lee	(NC 2001)
Dr Sheila Lee	(NC 1952)
Wing Sham Lee	(NC 2002)
Kate Lees	(NC 1982)
Sarah Maria Leiter	(NC 2008)
Veronica W F Leng	(NC 1975)
Julia Lennon	(NC 1996)
Rebecca Bek Ee Leong	(NC 1992)
Miss Sarah J Leverton	(NC 1995)
Patricia Lewis	(NC 2010)
Miss Kate Lidiard	(NC 1981)
Kang Hui Lim	(NC 1993)
Dr Carol Lim-Waller	(NC 1965)
Lyn Lindsay	(*Burgess* NC 1982)
June M Lindsey	(NC 1941)
Jane Lipton	(NC 1980)
Nicki Little	(*Lees* NC 1973)
Morag Loader	(NC 1983)
Mary Lomax	(*Winstanley* NC 1993)
Sarennah J P Longworth	(NC 1997)
Joanna Lootens	(*Vallat* NC 1993)
Danielle Lopes	(NC 2006)
Margaret Loseby Venzi	(NC 1958)
Miss Juliette Rosemary Losq	(NC 1997)
Denise Ann Love	(NC 1970)
Gillian Lovegrove	(*Lowther* NC 1961)
Betty Lowe	(NC 1951)
Dr Sam Lucy	(NC 1991)
Sandra Luscombe	(*Luff* NC 1965)
Susi Luss	(NC 1969)
Jenny Lynch	(NC 1983)
Dr Anne Lyon	(*Butland* NC 1967)
Dr Chaoying Ma	(NC 1988)
Fiona Maarhuis	(*Martin* NC 1959)
Felicity Macdonald-Smith	
Dr Jane MacDougall (Mrs Frost)	(NC 1976)
Jeanie (Jane) Macintosh	(NC 1942)
Esme Major	(NC 1989)
Baroness Mallalieu QC	(NC 1964)
Maria Mama-Timotheou	(NC 2007)
Dr Jenny Mander	(NC 1983)
Rosemary K Mann	(*Bayes* NC 1967)
Susan Manning	(*Valentine* NC 1973)
Lindsey Mansfield	(*Marshall* NC 1986)
Sally Mantell	(NC 2009)
Louise Marshall	(NC 2008)
Mrs Anne Martin	(NC 1956)
Lynda Martin Alegi	(*Watt* NC 1970)
Marguerite Mason	(*Chapman* NC 1944)
Anne Mathews	(*Wilcock* NC 1955)
Alexandra Matthew	(NC 2007)
Gabrielle Maughan	(*Green* NC 1973)
Nicola May	(*Dorey* NC 1993)
Katrina Blandy Mayson	(NC 1992)
Nel McDonald	(NC 2008)
Kathryn-Ann McEwen	(NC 2008)
Mary Barbara McHugo	(NC 1943)
Christine McIntosh	(*Murphy* NC 1979)
Nicola McMahon	(*Thompson* NC 2001)
Jane McMullan	(NC 1950)
Hannah McQuail	(NC 2008)
Serrie Meakins	(*Bampton* NC 1976)
Shefalika Mehta	(*Agarwal* NC 1986)
Barbara K Melrose	(*Southworth* NC 1970)
Pat Merriman	(NC 1944)
Domna Maria Michailidou	(NC 2008)
Laura Michel	(*Carruthers* NC 1995)
Naomi Elisabeth Emily Miles	(NC 2007)
Laura Miller	(NC 1989)
Celia P Milstein	(NC 1959)
Dr Julie Milton	(NC 1979)
Angela Minnery	(NC 1994)
Mary Mirchandani	(NC 1957)
Daisy Mitchell	(NC 2008)
Erin Mitchell	(NC 1991)
Dr Evelyn Joan Mitchell	(NC 1948)
Robyn Moates	(NC 2010)
Kiran Modha	(NC 1994)
Uzma Moeen	(NC 1998)
Louise Monaghan	(*Arter* NC 1990)
Alice Moncaster	(NC 1990)
Anna Montgomery	(NC 2007)
Lyndsey Ann Montgomery	(NC 2000)
Dr Dawn Moody	(NC 1986)
Judy Moody-Stuart	(*McLeary* NC 1960)
Alice Moore	(NC 2009)
Sheila More	(*Hull* NC 1947)
Christine Morgan	(*Glencross* NC 1962)
Nicola Morgan	(*Spencer* NC 1979)
Denise Morphet	(*Ereleigh* NC 1963)
Lucy Catherine Morrell	(NC 2009)
Miss M T Morrell	(NC 1955)
Roberta Morris	(NC 1981)
Tessa Morrison	(NC 1969)
Freya Morrissey	(NC 2005)
Beryl Mottershead	(NC 1948)
Lucy Mouland	(NC 1987)
Mrs Elizabeth Moyses	(*Jessop* NC 1974)
Catherine Mulgan	(*Gough* NC 1949)
Dr Barbara Murray	(*Wood* NC 1973)
Helen Mussell	(NC 2010)
Renuka Naidu	(NC 1961)
Kaoru Nasu-Tada	(NC 1995)
Kirsty Nathoo	(*Hall* NC 1998)
Lady (Anne-Marie) Nelson	(*Hall* NC 1960)
Divya Nelson	(NC 2009)
Jinty Nelson	(NC 1961)
Hannah Nesbit	(*Babor* NC 1993)
Judy Nesbit	(*Geake* NC 1977)
Margaret Neville	(NC 1940)
Lisa Newble	(NC 1998)
Elizabeth Siew-kuan Ng	(NC 1983)
Ivy Ng	(NC 1989)
Mary Nicholas	(NC 1944)
Claire Isobel O'Bryen Nichols	(NC 2010)
Alison M Nimmo	(NC 2005)
Gillian A Nimmo	(*Charlish* NC 1968)
Sally Norcross	(NC 1973)
Christine Northeast	(NC 1967)
Laura E Nottingham	(*Smith* NC 1971)
Jean Nuttall	(*Waterman* NC 1943)
Ailsa O'Brien	(NC 1944)
Gillian O'Mulloy	(NC 1975)
Baroness O'Neill of Bengarve	
Sally O'Neill	(NC 1980)
Dr Ruth M Odell	(*Licence* NC 1942)
Victoria Ogden	(NC 2010)
David and Caroline Ogle	
Nneka Okonta	(NC 1996)
Mary G Osborn	(*Keller* NC 1949)
Susanne Ottenstein	(*Landes* NC 1951)
Valerie Ovenden	(*Alsop* NC 1956)
Alexandra Owen	(NC 1996)
Susan J Owen	(NC 1973)
Jenny Owens	(NC 1955)
Hannah Pack	(NC 2009)
Dr Rachael Padman	
Mary M Page	(*Bowron* NC 1964)
Sheila G Page	(NC 1932)
Sally-Ann Paine	(*Turrell* NC 1984)
Joanna Palmer	(*Dobson* NC 1972)
Dr Julia Palmer	(NC 1975)
Selina Papa	(NC 1995)
Janet Elizabeth Parker	(NC 1989)
Margaret Parmée	(*Clarke* NC 1965)
Amy Parrish	(NC 2008)
Deepa Parry-Gupta	(NC 1987)
Sue Parsons	(NC 1988)
Professor Ivana K Partridge	(*Shott* NC 1972)
Fay Pascoe	(*Yelland* NC 1954)
Margaret Pateman	(*Lewis* NC 1960)
Sara Paterson-Brown	(NC 1978)
Beatrice Patrick	(NC 2009)
Mrs Carol Pearce	(*Ormerod* NC 1961)
Adèle Clare Pearson	(NC 2008)
Emma Pearson	(*Anderson* NC 1949)
Alice Peasgood	(NC 1982)
Hannah Pennicott	(NC 2009)
Heather Pentney	(*McCallum* NC 1984)
Louise Penton	(NC 2009)
Marcela Gómez Pérez	(NC 2004)
Pamela Sharp Perrott	(NC 1962)
Rosemary Pestell	(*Evans* NC 1965)
Ann Petrie	(*Young* NC 1957)
Hazel Petty	(*Day* NC 1983)
Dr Katie Petty-Saphon	(NC 1969)
Emma Pewsey	(NC 2006)
Mrs Alice Phillips	(NC 1979)
Diana Phillips	(*Hakim* NC 1948)
Roisin Pill	(*Riordan* NC 1960)
Cordelia Pilz	(*Harrison* NC 1985)
Pamela Pitcher	(*Heald* NC 1963)
Claire Plackett	(NC 1982)
Mary Playford	(*Dettmann* NC 1960)
Hannah Ruth Plews	(NC 1995)
Charlotte Pollock	(NC 2010)
Mrs Isabel Pooley	(*Mackley* NC 1995)
Jennifer Potter	(NC 1952)
Kirsty Potter	(NC 2007)
Cecilia Powell	(NC 1963)
Jenni Powell	(NC 2007)
Astrid von Preussen	(NC 2004)
Penny Price	(*Joyce* NC 1980)
Louise Pryor	(NC 1978)
Dr Laura Pugsley	(NC 1995)
Kate Pumfrey	(NC 2008)
Hannah Louise Punter	(NC 2010)
Patience Purdy	(*Fairbairn* NC 1948)
Claire Louise Purnell	(NC 1989)
Margaret Pyle	(*Pugh* NC 1952)
Dr Judy Quinn	
Angela Fagg Rackham	(NC 1964)

Mair D Rainbow (*Thomas* NC 1981)
Tamara Rajah (NC 1999)
Tara Rajah (NC 2002)
Dr Barbara J Randall (NC 1973)
Nandini Rao (NC 1982)
Catherine Rawson (NC 1975)
Madeleine Rea (NC 2007)
Mrs Mary Ream (NC 1943)
Jenny Reavell (*Etty-Leal* NC 1994)
Valery Rees (*Apley* NC 1965)
Caroline Renard Adamyk (NC 1982)
Jocelyn Rennie (NC 1956)
Elizabeth Renshaw (NC 1987)
Rebecca Revell (*Ireson* NC 1996)
Fiona Reynolds (NC 1976)
Susannah Reynoldson (*Madden* NC 1981)
Professor Dame Alison Richard (NC 1966)
Audrey Jarratt Richards (NC 1959)
Elizabeth Jane Richards (NC 2005)
Dr Jane Richards (*Canning* NC 1980)
Miss Kelly Richards (NC 1997)
Frances E A Riches (*Taylor* NC 1957)
Janet Riddlestone (*Warham* NC 1946)
Honor Ridout (NC 1967)
Marianne Rigby (NC 1991)
Susan Roberts (NC 1969)
Judy Robinson (*Griffiths* NC 1965)
Karen Robinson (NC 1996)
Val Robson (NC 1979)
Karen Rodgers (NC 1984)
Dr Pippa Rogerson (NC 1980)
Hilary Rosser (NC 1962)
Alison D Rowe (NC 1980)
Nancy Rowe (NC 2009)
Dr Valerie Rowe (*Walton* NC 1969)
Heather Rowland (*Kearsley* NC 1964)
Joan Rudd-Jones (*Newhouse* NC 1943)
Antonia Ruppel (NC 1998)
Heather Ann Russell (*Brown* NC 1957)
Judith M Russell (NC 1974)
Rachel Russell (NC 2009)
Lynsey Russell-Watts (NC 1999)
Katie Rutter (NC 1984)
Sonia P M Ryder (*Meldrum* NC 1957)
Enid M Sage (*Hirst* NC 1950)
Victoria Salem (NC 1979)
Frances K H Salter (NC 2001)
Betty Sandars (*Yielder* NC 1961)
Dr Alison Sansome (*Rhind* NC 1982)
Charmaine Saw (NC 1990)
Catherine Anne Sayer (NC 2008)
Betty Schofield (NC 1938)
A Scrase Dickins (*Moller* NC 1952)
Freda Sedgwick (NC 1975)
Heather Self (*Dowdeswell* NC 1977)
Carol Sergeant CBE (*Hawksworth* NC 1971)
Catherine Seville (NC 1984)
Tessa Karin Gisela Seymour (*Salmons* NC 1992)
Diane Seymour-Williams (*Wilson* NC 1978)
Margaret Shamy (*Davies* NC 1951)
Dr Ruth Verity Sharman (NC 1972)
Anne Sharpley (NC 1968)

Jialin Shen (NC 2005)
Janet Simkin (NC 1975)
Francesca Simon (*Fortescue Hitchins* NC 1972)
Kirsti Simonsuuri (NC 1971)
Mrs Ruth Simpson (*Bonney* NC 1953)
Gaylen Sinclair (NC 2010)
Sally Singer (*Scott* NC 1995)
Mrs Kavita Singh (*Bhasin* NC 1986)
Victoria Singh (*Markham* NC 1971)
Patricia H Sledge (NC 1951)
Carolyn Smith (*Buckley* NC 1968)
Claire Smith (*Whimster* NC 1980)
Deborah Smith (*Freeman* NC 1977)
Dr Debra Smith (NC 1974)
Frances Smith (NC 2007)
Helen Christina Smith (NC 2010)
Dr Meredith A Smith (NC 1993)
Vicki C Smith (NC 1985)
Victoria Smith (*Browne* NC 1973)
Victoria Smith (NC 2005)
Sally Laurence Smyth (*Coussins* NC 1971)
Miriam Solomon (NC 1976)
Michaela Southworth (*Brown* NC 1994)
Patricia Southworth (*James* NC 1961)
Weronika Magdalena Sowa (NC 2010)
Jennifer Spence (NC 1979)
Annette Spencer (*Wrigley* NC 1988)
Gillian Spencer (*Chapman* NC 1949)
Maggie Spencer (NC 1971)
Rosemary Spencer (*Stewartson* NC 1967)
Sally E Spink (*Jones* NC 1995)
Jay Springham (NC 2008)
Chloe Squires (NC 2003)
Karen Staartjes (NC 1975)
Erin Stafford (NC 2010)
Isabel Stanley (*Gaylor* NC 1955)
Jenny Staples (*Lester* NC 1965)
Glenys Stead (*Thomas* NC 1965)
Helen Steers Mardinian (NC 1981)
Gillian Stein (*Matthews* NC 1946)
Dr Siân E Goldthorpe Stein (NC 1984)
Nina-Juliane Steinke (NC 2005)
Emily Stennett (NC 2008)
Gillian M Stevens (NC 1957)
Clare Stevenson-Hamilton (*Pooley* NC 1988)
Janet Stewart (*Wilson* NC 1978)
Anne Stimson (NC 1968)
Caroline Alexandra Stocks (NC 2008)
The Stocks Family
Hilda M M Stoneley (*Cox* NC 1950)
Susan J Stoughton-Harris (NC 1976)
Lucy Stoy (NC 1998)
Kathryn Strachan (*Duncan* NC 1976)
Andy Strakova (NC 2010)
Lady Strange (NC 1984)
Alan T Street
Jennifer Stroud (*Stephenson* NC 1963)
Ann Stuart (*Wittrick* NC 1969)
Dr Jacqueline Elizabeth Summers (NC 1987)
Lu Sun (NC 2007)
Alice M Sunderland (NC 1998)
Ann Sutcliffe (*Robinson* NC 1979)

Mary Swingler (*Goodwin* NC 1971)
Joy W M Tan (NC 1988)
Joanna C Tapp (NC 2003)
May C Targett (NC 1956)
Deborah Tayler (*Bryde* NC 1968)
Lee Taylor (*Metcalfe* NC 1990)
Pamela Taylor (*Higson* NC 1964)
Dr Virginia Taylor (NC 1970)
Mary Taylour (*Mauger* NC 1947)
Hilary Temple (*Aston* NC 1943)
Gillian Tennant (NC 1949)
Ada Ee Der Teo (NC 2009)
Dr Berrak Teymur (NC 1997)
Ellen Rose Thomas (NC 2010)
Joanna Thomas (*Cawood* NC 1981)
Amy Thompson (*Healey* NC 2000)
Emma Thompson (NC 1978)
Anne Thomson
Judith Jarvis Thomson (NC 1950)
Rachel Marianne Sarah Thorley (NC 2008)
Charlie Thorne (NC 2010)
Antonia Till (*Clapham* NC 1957)
Angela Tjay Mazuri (*Grady* NC 1981)
Judith A Todd-Copley (NC 1969)
Etain Todds (*Kabraji* NC 1948)
Christy Toh (NC 1994)
Ruth Toulson (NC 1996)
Harriet Trayler-Clarke (NC 2008)
Mary Tredennick (NC 1952)
Dr Alison Trevor (NC 1980)
Jackie Tubis (*Dupere* NC 1973)
Nicolina Turcan (NC 2010)
Sarah Grace Turner (NC 2001)
Anna Tweed (NC 2007)
Cherry Tweed (*Moore* NC 1976)
Florence Tyler (NC 2008)
Mary Tyler (*Hall* NC 1979)
Alexis M Tymon (NC 2010)
Sidney Tyrrell (*Welsh* NC 1966)
Dr Yvonne Underhill (*Terry* NC 1975)
Lucie Unitt (*Johnstone* NC 2000)
Jenny Urwin (NC 1987)
Rakhee Vaja (NC 2009)
Julie Laura Mary Valk (NC 2006)
Melissa Van Doorselaer (NC 2010)
Jenny Vince (*Smith* NC 1975)
Elizabeth Voak (*Caffrey* NC 1968)
Marina Vraila (NC 1982)
Maja Vukovic (NC 2003)
Vivian Wade (NC 1980)
San-Toi Wagner (*Wan* NC 1987)
Sue Wagstaffe (NC 1977)
Julie Wakefield (NC 1984)
Anna Wakerley (NC 1976)
Fiona Walkinshaw (NC 1982)
Emily Walsh (NC 2008)
Elisabeth Walwyn (NC 1957)
Xin Wang (NC 2005)
Annie Warburton (NC 1988)
Sarah Ward (NC 1960)
Rachel Warden (NC 1949)
Dr Rachel Warren (NC 1982)

Dr Panit Watcharawitch (NC 1999)
Sarah Watling (NC 2008)
Olivia M Watson (NC 2010)
Helen Webb (NC 2003)
Jean Frances Webb (*Moon* NC 1953)
Ann Webbley (*East* NC 1968)
Ivy Webster (*Garlick* NC 1948)
Lucy R Wedderburn (NC 1979)
Truda Weiler (*Woollen* NC 1944)
Miss Y E Weir (NC 1942)
Sarah Wellings (NC 1991)
Lourina Pretorius West (NC 2002)
Meg Weston Smith (NC 1952)
Charlotte Westwood-Dunkley (NC 1984)
Dr Nicky Whitaker (NC 1970)
Anna White (*Meddins* NC 1990)
Norma White (NC 1960)
Fiona Whitehurst (*Baker* NC 1986)
Molly Whittington-Egan (NC 1956)
Emma Widdowson (*Senior* NC 1996)
Patricia Wightman (*Taylor* NC 1962)
Evelyn Wilcock (*Gollin* NC 1958)
Dr C Deborah Wilde (NC 1972)
Sarah Wilder (*Dowden* NC 1998)
Mrs Rita Wilkinson (NC 1944)
Sarah Lee Wilkinson (NC 1994)
Rosalind M Willatts (NC 1963)
Joyce Willcocks (*Warman* NC 1953)
Anne Williams (NC 1977)
Professor Faith M Williams (*Wright* NC 1963)
Ruth Williams (NC 1953)
Susan Williams (*Walpole* NC 1979)
Virginia Williams (*Carey* NC 1963)
Gill Williamson (*Anderson Smith* NC 1946)
Dr Audrey S Willis (NC 1937)
Claire Wilson (NC 1983)
Sarah L Wilson (NC 1985)
Tina Wilson (*Nixon* NC 1959)
Sarah Winfield (NC 2007)
Mary Juliet Winteler (NC 1968)
Antonia Wise (*Sidley* NC 1984)
Sonia M Withers (*Lechem* NC 1942)
Joanna Withers (*Gurney* NC 1984)
Cindy Wai Chi Wong (NC 2002)
Emily Woodhouse (NC 2008)
Diana Wright (*Bramwell* NC 1948)
Joanna Wright (*Setchell* NC 1976)
Kelly Wright (NC 1995)
Rosemary Yallop (*Moore* NC 1976)
Angie C Y Yan (NC 2010)
Wendy Ann Yates (NC 1965)
Dr Crystal Jing Jing Yeo (NC 2005)
Sharon S F Yeoh (NC 1992)
Fiona Yeomans (*Main* NC 1975)
Deepika Yerrakalva (NC 2000)
Carol Bik Kay Yip (NC 1993)
Dr Gill Yudkin (*Isaacs* NC 1961)
Fiona Zealley (*Cooper* NC 1981)
Yimao Zhang (NC 2011)